In some corner of a foreign field

Imagine a marching column, four abreast, stretching 500 miles from the Cenotaph in London back to Aberdeen: it would take six days without pause before the rearguard reached Whitehall. This image attempts to represent the number of men from the United Kingdom and Commonwealth who died fighting overseas in the 20th century. Around 170 miles of that line – 574,863 men – lie in named graves in France. The 1924 plaque (left) in Bayeux Cathedral reminds us that in the Great War (1914–18) half a million men – another 150 miles of the line – have no named grave. In the Second World War the number of missing would be far fewer, but another 600,000 soldiers, sailors and airmen died worldwide. The 20th century left 2,917 British and Commonwealth burial grounds in French soil.

A civilization can be measured by how it treats its war dead. The British and Commonwealth tradition shares with the United States the principle of equality in death, regardless of race, rank or creed, and the creation of perpetual places of remembrance and honour. Lord Charles Oliver Fitzroy, 21, Lieutenant in the Grenadier Guards (grave reference: 8.B.18), son of the Duke of Grafton, has the same treatment in death as Azeour Ulla of the Muslim faith, an oiler in the boiler room of the SS *City of Florence* (16.B.10). But in contrast to American tradition, there would be no repatriation

for Com⸺ ⸺ ⸺
on monu⸺ ⸺
and his sa⸺ ⸺
his unit, his ⸺

No war⸺ ⸺ ⸺
during the ye⸺ ⸺ ⸺ ⸺ Bayeux. Corporal Eric⸺ ⸺ (⸺ page 15) worked here in No.32 Graves ⸺gistration Unit and a selection of his unofficial photographs of the Bayeux Cemetery taking shape, found buried during building work in the village of Castillon in 2005, are published here for the first time. The largest Commonwealth war cemetery of the Second World War in France stands as a microcosm of the truly gigantic enterprise that began in 1914 under the inspiration of the Commonwealth War Graves Commission's founder, Sir Fabian Ware (1869–1949), whose name was given to the permanent bypass that determined the site of the permanent cemetery.

This account is based upon interviews with and the personal experiences of men and women, British and French, who had dealings with death. Death struck unquietly and haphazardly, and those who had to deal with its consequences had a grim and inglorious mission: as the German conscript and novelist Erich Maria Remarque (1898–1970) declared, 'Death is not an adventure to those who come face to face with it.'

The Army Graves Registration Unit tapes out and digs the first graves in the large field belonging to Monsieur Léon Gautier, *agriculteur*, opposite the civilian cemetery on the Littry road west of Bayeux.

'We, once conquered by William, have returned to set free his native land.'

THE MEMORIAL TO THE MISSING, BAYEUX

Bayeux: liberation

It is 9 a.m., Wednesday 7 June 1944. The people (above) have drifted down the main streets and gathered at the central crossroads in Bayeux near the old Fish Market (the present Tourist Office) in quiet expectation (see also aerial reconnaissance picture, page 11 inset, taken at the same time and showing the crowd forming). The Germans pulled out overnight, and the only news is by word of mouth – and some clandestine radios. But tricolor flags were coming out into the open, and

André Maurice, Eric Gunton's future lifelong photographic assistant, has brought his camera to capture this extraordinary moment. In a few minutes the first British soldiers, their faces blackened and with branches still in their helmet netting, will appear down the Rue Maréchal Foch and the Rue de la Cave on bicycles, along with a few tracked vehicles, and, later, Sherman tanks, smothered in flowers. Momentarily stunned by the implications of what was unfolding, the people of Bayeux soon gave way to cheering, applause, embraces, and much crying. They were free, without loss, damage or disturbance. The *résistance* could come into the open: the four-year nightmare of occupation and humiliation was over. After this wave of joy (and a brief moment of panic in the afternoon when it was thought the Germans might be returning and the flags were snatched back through the windows!) collaborationists could be removed and legitimacy restored.

Thirty metres from the Fish Market, at 140 Rue Saint Jean, were the offices of the collaborationist 'Legion of French Volunteers against the Bolsheviks' (LVF). On 8 June 1944 the offices would quietly be dismantled (opposite, top). Set up in the high street on 22 May 1942, working-class French volunteers (their average age was 24) were tempted into the SS to fight on the Eastern Front. Six weeks before, the latest batch, on their way to Russia, had been blessed and absolved of their sins by the Cardinal Archbishop of Paris. Few returned.

> 7 June 1944: Mlle Jeanette Bouve (now Madame Ratel), age 19 in 1944, shared lodgings on the third floor at 56 Rue Saint Malo, the street in the picture (above), with fellow corsetière Mlle Marie-Thérèse d'Helft. Madame Ratel recalls: 'All was quiet, and it was a wonderful sunny morning. We went down to fetch some bread and, being curious, heard some shouts and cries, so ran on down to the bottom of the street just as the English soldiers started arriving, their faces all blackened up, looking tired. Straightway there was a reception committee of wine and cider, the flags came out, flowers were showered onto them. Everyone was so happy, everyone was laughing.'

In the days and weeks to come, the joy and relief of liberation was tempered by an awareness communicated by the flood of refugees of the great sacrifice among military and civilian alike that was being played out on their doorstep. The centre of Tilly, for example, although only another 13kms (8 miles) further inland, was already destroyed before Bayeux was liberated. So also was Caen, Saint-Lô, Lisieux, Vire, Condé sur Noireau, and many other towns besides.

Bayeux tripled its population and became a vital centre for refugees, for Army administration and supply, for communications, for hospitalization and hospitality, for 'rest and recuperation'. With good cause, the local people later spoke of 'la ville miraculée' (the miraculously saved town).

8 June 1944: 'In Bayeux, as elsewhere, collaborators rubbed shoulders with resistance fighters … a few women, set up in houses, were subject to health checks and served the enemy. Some young men joined the LVF, whose offices were in the Rue Saint Jean. On liberation, the collaborators were made to walk along the high street: men like Darnal, but also others, who were more unexpected, probably members of Action Française. The young women had their heads shaved.'

MLLE ROLANDE DUBOIS
(MADAME HUET), AGE 25
IN 1944

Keep right! In the Rue Saint Jean the British look askance at their ally, so much better paid and turned out. The Hôtel Lion d'Or became a convivial club for senior officers and British journalists: Montgomery had a table permanently set aside there.

'Bayeux was a rest centre for the troops of the line. Men in uniform crowded its narrow pavements, American blacks from the Deep South rubbing shoulders with Irish Guards, Canadians and Poles; its little shops tempted us with perfume, silk stockings, apple tarts and trashy jewellery. The troops' spell away from the fighting was brief so there was always a good deal of merry-making in Bayeux, with cider, cognac and Calvados.'

SISTER BRENDA MCBRYDE, AGE 25 IN 1944

> '**In the midst of life we are in death ...**'
> THE BOOK OF COMMON PRAYER

The battlefield graves

It was the men's comrades, supervised by 'burial officers' chosen within their units, who were expected to bury their own dead; as appropriate for each of the armed services, their Commanding Officer would write to the next of kin. The burial returns were written out in triplicate, going up the chain of command from the burial party to the 'burial officer' (often a platoon lieutenant or adjutant) who collated the information and fed it back to the appropriate authorities so that the Graves Registration Units (GRUs) could come back into the field and register the graves by marking them. Later still the Graves Concentration Units (GCUs) would disinter the remains – a task often carried out by French labourers under a British officer's supervision.

But during the battle itself it was a deeply harrowing experience for the soldiers and officers to bury men they had known well, men with whom they had formed intense bonds of comradeship unknown to those outside military life.

Inverted rifles stuck in the ground by the bayonet indicated that a body had been checked and awaited burial: but it could take many days before it was possible to reach the bodies safely, by which time the un-buried comrades presented an alarming and disagreeable aspect – 'grotesque waxwork figures' as one officer put it.

Booby traps, along with unexploded ordnance and mines, were ever-present risks for those tasked with recovering the dead, even after the war was well over.

Commanding Officers sometimes refused to allow their men to handle corpses or body parts blown into the hedgerows because of the effect on morale; at other times, men freshly landed and green to combat were detailed this grim work to accustom them to the prospect of the greater horror of doing the same for men they knew.

Photographs of British war dead are few and far between. This picture shows how men were normally buried, still in their boots, wrapped and tied in Army blankets.

On 30 November 1944 the men of No.48 Royal Marine Commando killed on D-Day and buried in this former garden in Saint Aubin were concentrated to Bayeux. The bodies of 23-year-old Captain Frederick Charles Laurence Lennard and 22-year-old Lieutenant Thomas David Yates are now in Plot 14.A.23 and 19 with their men, as here, alongside.

Two bodies recovered from the battlefield lie in a handcart near the village of Cristot.

'The second time we went up there [to Lebisey Wood] I had to clear all our dead up from the first encounter after they had lain there for four or five weeks with booby traps on them.'
LANCE CORPORAL E. SEAMAN, STRETCHER BEARER

'Saw lorryloads of the dead brought in, I can see them now, all higgledy-piggledy inside, rolled into khaki blankets and tightly tied up with string, each labelled with their name, number and regiment, their shoes sticking out. Once they brought in some Germans – you could tell from their boots. Some came from Caen, but a lot were brought in from around Tilly directly from the battlefield. Both my brothers worked in the temporary cemetery for the military hospital a kilometre away [see inverted 'L' halfway between 3a and the railway line on page 10] and in the main cemetery.'
JEAN LEDOLLEY, AGE 16 IN 1944, LIVED IN THE FARM CLOSEST TO THE FUTURE BAYEUX CEMETERY AND WITNESSED A P47 THUNDERBOLT CRASH INTO THE NEIGHBOURING FIELD ON D-DAY, KILLING THE AMERICAN PILOT

'Went to recce situation ref. Sgt Bartle – through fields into copse. No sign of him. Trooper Lynwood still lying there – it worries me. On the way back DW's [the Duke of Wellington's regiment's] officer asked me if I would bury two chaps killed a week ago in the attack on Cristot. Seemingly 4th/7th men [of the Royal Dragoon Guards] lying in ditch ever since. Really unpleasant – crawling. Scrounged some blankets and started to tie them up. DW's officer went away to be sick and did not return until I had finished. DW's had dug graves for me and I read funeral service – then violently sick myself.'
LESLIE SKINNER, PADRE ATTACHED TO THE SHERWOOD RANGERS, 22 JUNE 1944

'I saw a line of soldiers in uniform, feet towards me. Slowly I walked along searching. Sometimes I had to step between them to get a better look at a face, half turned away, or a regimental insignia that was partly obscured. None of them appeared to be grossly mutilated. No separate messes here: officers rubbed shoulders with privates, a sergeant-major with a corporal. All had the same waxen pallor, some eyes were closed, some open, all unseeing. At last, I had found one of the lads – old Harry …. I touched him. He was icy cold, and somewhat rigid. Carefully I removed one of his identity discs. I did it as if he were asleep and I didn't want to waken him. I stood before him for a few seconds. I didn't pray. I didn't think. It wasn't homage really, just a sort of "cheerio Harry".'
CORPORAL JOHN CROPPER, A TANK COMMANDER IN THE 24TH LANCERS AND LATER THE SHERWOOD RANGERS, SENT TO IDENTIFY SOME DEAD COMRADES

'Before the invasion I can remember passing his office door and I saw he'd just received an issue of crosses and they were piled in a corner and it gave one a very nasty turn, I can tell you, and I walked quickly by: poor old padre, his equipment for the invasion was a pile of white crosses.'

CAPTAIN JOHN SEMKEN

The Army chaplains

God was important to the generation of 1944, and in the vital task of keeping track of who had died and where, officers in the front line, and the GRUs in the rear, were greatly helped by the chaplains. Alongside the fighting men, they recovered the wounded, performed the last rites to the dying, and gave Christian burial in the battlefield – often at great risk. They performed the same task for the enemy dead.

The chaplains were expected to complete casualty lists, burial returns, and grasp identification and registration procedures. They were supposed to take ink fingerprints – if possible – before burial and forward them, along with any personal effects (a watch, a ring maybe), parcelled and labelled, to the GRUs. Such work fulfilled a heartfelt need among the men for their dead to be reverently buried. Chaplains, like the senior officers, also had the grievous task at the end of

almost every day of writing 'casualty letters' to next of kin, who did not always take kindly to such a communication.

The Reverend Skinner, 8th Armoured Brigade, attached to the Sherwood Rangers, arrived in Bayeux on 7 June. His diary gives a stark and detailed account of how he worked. Recovering crew from burnt out tanks was particularly horrible. On 4 August he noted: '8 men killed, 5 still in tanks. Went back to start line then forward along C Squadron axis. Buried the three dead and tried to reach the remaining dead in tanks still too hot and burning. Place absolute shambles. Infantry dead and some Germans lying around. Horrible mess. Fearful job picking up bits and pieces and reassembling for identification and putting in blankets for burial. Squadron Leader offered to lend me some men to help. Refused. The less men who live and fight in tanks have

'When I came on duty at daybreak the Resuscitation Officer met me in the Operating Theatre. "Have a Padre in. Been trying to get him in shape all night. No response. He was out burying the dead when he got caught up in some mortar fire. Right thigh shattered near the hip joint. Compound fracture of the left lower leg. Pretty desperate but if you get that right thigh off he might react." He finally died on the fifth day.'

CANADIAN MILITARY SURGEON MAJOR JOHN BURWELL HILLSMAN M.D.

A chaplain performs the burial rites before a Royal Army Medical Corps ambulance near Ryes, named as a British cemetery on the same day as Bayeux. The spire of Bazenville church can just be seen through the trees.

The heat of August made it vital to carry out burials promptly. At Hottot les Bagues, wooden crosses are being painted with the details of Private Bernard England, 19 (5.B.6), Captain Robert Evans, 28 (5.B.2) and Lance Serjeant Frederick Maddocks, 24 (5.B.3), of the Durham Light Infantry, killed in action on 9 August. Before a big attack the Pioneers would distribute crosses to where burial parties were expected — little encouragement for the young soldiers about to go into action.

'Hardest of all was the impossibility of giving complete detail. Having dealt with the remains of a body blown to pieces either in the tank or on a minefield, it was possible truthfully to say their boy had died instantly without suffering. If they wrote back — as some did — wanting to know how I could be sure that he had not suffered, replying was not easy.'

PADRE LESLIE SKINNER

to do with this side of things the better. They know it happens but to force it on their attention is not good. My job. This was more than normally sick-making. Really ill — vomiting. Buried all five in 43 Div cemetery being set up at the crossroads in Berjou.'

When there was only ash inside the stricken tank, the only surviving identifiable element might be the pelvic bones, their position suggesting who had been the driver, the co-driver (who was also the machine-gunner) alongside him in the lowest part of the hull, the radio-operator to the left of the gunner in the turret, and the tank commander on the command bridge at the back of the turret. However it is not uncommon in British and Commonwealth cemeteries to see communal graves, where a tank, armoured vehicle or aircraft crew are reburied together because of the nature of the remains when found: examples include 27.F.1–3 (tanks) and 28.J.16–19 (aircraft).

'It had been a tough night. I had earned a rest. As I walked wearily towards my tent, I saw a fresh mound of earth in the field and the Padre placing ropes around a blanket-draped form. I remembered the boy and felt miserable. I went over. It was the least I could do now. The service began. Men slowly drifted around and took off their berets. I looked at their faces. This soldier was not alone. He had many friends. They didn't know his name but he was a friend. I glanced at the road and saw some French peasants standing with their heads bowed. They crossed themselves. The boy was lowered gently and reverently into the grave. The service ended. All left except two pioneers. I waited until he was covered. The pioneers shaped the mound of earth: they did it so carefully. It must look nice. Poor kid, all by yourself in the corner of a French field. Well, you'll soon have plenty of company ....'

MAJOR HILLSMAN AT SECQUEVILLE, AFTER AN UNSUCCESSFUL OPERATION ON A CANADIAN SOLDIER

The cutting edge

Of the men brought in to field hospitals, 93 per cent would survive. A great tribute is owed to those in the medical services who saved so many in the most difficult of circumstances and thereby kept the cemeteries smaller than they might have otherwise been. In the front line were the Casualty Clearance and Field Dressing Stations. In the Field Surgical Units were those deemed too seriously wounded for removal to the rear, and who had to be operated upon without delay. The military surgeons frequently had to operate in camouflaged canvas theatres set up in bare, open fields, with their own generators but in the strictest blackout conditions – and often working within range of the enemy guns. They could, in exceptional circumstances, find themselves cutting, sewing and staunching for 36 hours without relief.

From 10 July Major Hillsman operated at Secqueville, now, like Ryes, one of the smaller Commonwealth war cemeteries in Normandy. He dedicated his book *11 Men and a Scalpel* 'to the hundreds of patient and uncomplaining soldiers who passed through my Unit' and describes in moving terms his experience: 'We operated in Secqueville for ten days, and covered the attack that took Caen. During those days we became veterans. We saw tragic sights from which we were never to be free for ten long months. Men with heads shattered, and grey, dirty brains oozing out from the jagged margins of skull bones. Youngsters with holes in their chests fighting for air and breathing with a ghastly sucking noise. Soldiers with intestines draining faeces into their belly walls, and with their guts churned into a bloody mess by high explosives. Legs that were dead and stinking – but still wore a muddy shoe. Operating floors that had to be scrubbed with Lysol to rid them of the stench of dead flesh. Red blood that flowed over while life held on by the slender thread of time. Boys who came to you with a smile and died on the operating table. Boys who lived long enough for you to learn their name and then were carried away in trucks piled high with the dead. We became the possessors of bitter knowledge no man has ever been able to describe.'

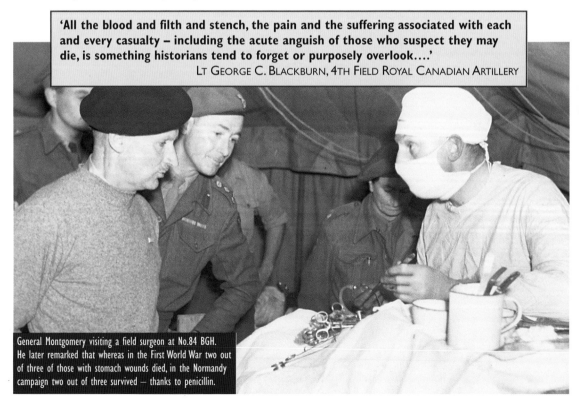

General Montgomery visiting a field surgeon at No.84 BGH. He later remarked that whereas in the First World War two out of three of those with stomach wounds died, in the Normandy campaign two out of three survived — thanks to penicillin.

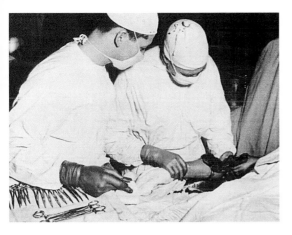

New operation techniques and surgical instruments during the Second World War, together with the liberal use of penicillin as it became available in quantity in 1944, slashed the proportion of deaths among the wounded compared to the 1914–18 war. In this case the surgeon and his assistant were unable to save the man's arm and had to proceed to amputation to save his life.

Not all were able to take the strain: 35-year-old Captain Franklyn Holt Lloyd (I. F. 26) of the Royal Army Medical Corps, shot himself on 20 July. In her book *A Nurse's War*, Brenda McBryde, serving in No.75 British General Hospital, reported the incident: 'Deeply involved as we all were with the wounded men in our care, no one noticed that one of the medical staff was under strain. At first light, one misty morning, a stretcher bearing a body draped in a Union Jack was carried from the medical officers' tents. Major MacPherson had shared a tent with Capt. Lloyd and had been awakened by the shot. He was shaken now and bitterly self-critical. How was it possible to share a tent with a man and not know he had this on his mind? But we had all been too busy with our own jobs to stand back and look about us. No one had realised that Capt. Lloyd, a true physician, had been overwhelmed by a sense of failure amongst the need for so much surgery....'

26 June 1944: the wounded on stretchers are loaded onto a waiting Royal Army Medical Corps ambulance for evacuation from the battlefield to a Casualty Clearing Station.

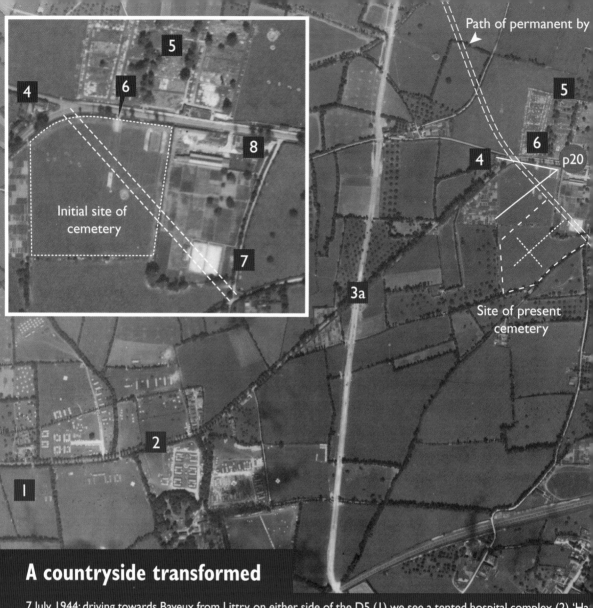

Path of permanent by

Initial site of cemetery

Site of present cemetery

p20

A countryside transformed

7 July 1944: driving towards Bayeux from Littry, on either side of the D5 (1) we see a tented hospital complex (2). 'Ha Street', as the road was known, takes us across the oil pipelines and temporary bypass (3a) – opened today – and at (4 the road bends (see house pages 20 and 27) and runs past the walled Western Communal (civilian) Cemetery (5). The entrance to the provisional military cemetery (6) is opposite (see inset above). There are tennis courts nearby (7), soo to be demolished by the path of a new, permanent bypass. Driving past the sheds of the Lesage tombstone factory (8) (see pages 22 and 24) we reach the old porcelain factory (9). On the right, beyond a field and small wood, is the long r line and spire of the Benedictine nunnery (10) (see pages 14 and 27). Turn left into the Place du Château, and with the sub-prefecture (11) (see page 25) on the right, head for the cathedral (12). Behind it, the Rue Larcher takes us to the f market (13) where the first British troops arrived on 7 June (see inset top right showing French waiting at the crossroads). Double back past No.35 Rue Larcher (14) (Le Petit Normand restaurant in 2006), Gunton's future photography shop, and the Villa Bon Accueil (15), No.32 GRU's HQ (later expanded into the site of the present Tapest coach park), and along the road and bridge over the River Aure (16) (see page 14) to the undamaged railway station (To the east are the earthmovers advancing the new permanent bypass (18). Head out of town to rejoin the temporar bypass (3b), where a long trail of trucks (see inset right), soon reaching 3,500 a day, is coming in the other direction fo the final push onto Caen. Go over the Bailey bridge nicknamed 'Pangbourne' (19) on the River Aure to the junction w the Saint-Lô road and back towards town, over the Cherbourg-Caen railway line by means of another new Bailey brid (20) that replaced the stone bridge bombed on D-Day and re-opened to road traffic yesterday.

7 June 1944

13

p3b

p3t

13

9

10

11

12

14

15

16

p15

17

18

19

3b

N

Figures in red circles
denote page references

Quiet heroines

On 16 and 17 June 1944, five British General Hospitals (Nos. 79, 81, 84, 86 and 88) were landed in 'kit' form; the 50 nurses with No.75 BGH, who had set out from Southampton on 19 June under lowering skies, had to ride out the famous three-day storm at sea, and landed on the night of 22/23 June, along with Nos.20 and 77 BGH. The safest place for a concentration of hospitals in the tiny beachhead was deemed to be west of Bayeux; and on 24 June the lorries set out for the site which four days later was already working beyond its planned capacity. By 7 July they had already received over 2,000 patients, but the first death at the hospital complex was not until 12 July, the first burial the next day (Private Douglas Schofield, 20, Plot A:1:1). No.75 BGH, coming in behind the others, was still setting up when the aerial photograph on the previous page was taken. The big push onto Caen was under way, and the BGHs received an overspill of Canadian casualties. The turnover in the 600-bedded tented encampment peaked on 18 July, when 446 wounded were admitted – and 328 post-operative cases evacuated from No.75 BGH alone. The rule was: 'resuscitate, operate, evacuate', but you could be evacuated for relatively small ailments such as septic fingers – or even haemorrhoids!

Plot 1 begin to fill (see page 14), and 638 fatalities eventually came out of 'Harley Street' (see page 10), among them 149 German POWs and 15 Poles. The hospital returns (now in the National Archive) make grim reading. Among the Poles, for example, 23-year-old

The Army battledress was chemically impregnated to repel lice, which made it highly irritating to the skin, but was more practical for the demands of front-line nursing than the sisters' usual uniform.

Gunner Bazyll Sidoruk (16.A.7), a radio operator, was wounded in the abdomen while in his tank on 16 August at Jort; he was brought in, 'did well then collapsed and died. COD [Cause of death]: Broncho Pneumonia'. Lance Corporal Franciszek Gilewski, 38, (16.A.12) found his own solution to the stress of battle: on 18 August he was 'Admitted in a coma. Intoxicated. Did not regain consciousness. No post mortem arranged'.

No more graphic example of how nursing sisters saved lives can be cited than that of two nurses, Sister Dorothy Field and Sister Molly Evershed, who died together on board a ship returning with casualties from the Battle of Falaise to the safety of England.

Corporal Eric Gunton has captured a rare moment of relaxation — the nurses are not in their usual battledress but in the splendid full uniform of the Queen Alexandra's Imperial Military Nursing Service (QAIMNS), and the men in their 'walking out' uniforms of the Royal Army Medical Corps: one of the men is clearly amusing the audience. The presence of the civilian in the black hat suggests that the battle — or indeed the war — is over, and that the tents are no longer serving the wounded — but drinks!

This colour photograph of a Queen Alexandra nurse was taken at one of the Field Hospitals in August 1944 by a Captain Malindine.

Both nurses are recorded on the Memorial of the Missing of the Battle of Normandy, opposite the cemetery (panel 19, column 1 and panel 27), along with the 55 wounded men, 10 medical staff and 30 crew members, including Assistant Steward Fred Easteal, 51, (2.E.15), who were also lost in the tragedy.

> '**The *Amsterdam* is a smashing ship.
> At last I can make a worthwhile
> contribution to the war.**'
>   SISTER MOLLY EVERSHED IN A LETTER HOME

'The hospital carrier *Amsterdam* had already made two cross-Channel trips with patients and was midway on her third on 7 August when she struck a mine. One half of the vessel was completely wrecked and all in the engine room were lost. As many as possible of her full load of casualties were helped to safety, and the Sister-in-Charge, Miss Dorothy Anyta Field, QAIMNS, was already in the lifeboat when she realised that many helpless men who were still below decks would have to be abandoned. She insisted on returning to the ship, even as it began to settle in the water, and climbed back on board accompanied by one of her staff, Sister Molly Evershed.

In all, the two Sisters brought 75 men from the ward below decks to safety, returning for more after each one was delivered over the ship's rail, even though they knew that at any minute the stricken vessel could plummet to the bottom of the sea. The last to be brought up was a man whose leg had been amputated just before the mine exploded.

No longer able to walk upright because of the angle of the deck, the two Sisters went below for what was to be their last trip. In a final convulsion the sea closed over the *Amsterdam*, its patients, and the two women who gave their lives in their service. There was a fleeting image before the ship disappeared from sight of sturdy Molly Evershed trying in vain to squeeze her hips through a porthole. She was 27 years old and had recently become engaged to marry an Engineer. Miss Field was 32. 75 grateful men wrote to the parents of the two women, who were posthumously "Mentioned in Dispatches".'

  SISTER BRENDA MCBRYDE

> '... that we may wander o'er this bloody field
> To book our dead, and then to bury them.'
>
> WILLIAM SHAKESPEARE, *HENRY V*

Grave registration

The Army Graves Registration Units' tasks were to go out into the battlefield, record the provisional burials and ensure the graves were properly marked by a cross stamped with 'GRU' on the back. This indicated that the grave had been officially registered and was not to be touched by anyone else. The GRUs also had to choose appropriate sites for permanent cemeteries. Many of the men supervising these units had fought in the First World War and were highly decorated, and many came to see this work as a vocation more than an Army chore. In the Battle of Normandy there were five such units for the British, and two for the Canadians. In London, the man to whom they ultimately answered – Sir Fabian Ware – was also in charge of the Imperial War Graves Commission, but the IWGC could do no more than advise until such time as the burials by the Army into permanent cemeteries were complete – a process that would take at least four years.

This photograph was taken around 20 July 1944, the permanent bypass now under construction. Plot I is taking shape, with makeshift crosses. French civilians have been taken on, supervised by Corporal Rene Parsons, seen here standing at the back, far right, wearing glasses.

Many of the photographs in this book were taken by Corporal Eric Gunton (1903–78), seen in this 1945 picture holding some of his prints.

On 19 November 1944 he was allowed to return to South London on leave: six days later a V2 fell on Woolworths in New Cross, packed with Saturday shoppers, killing 168 and wounding 122, many of them children. 'I lost my father and several members of my family and my friends; I saw 80 people killed by a single bomb one evening in London. There are 28,000 British dead in Normandy: we have no right to forget.'

Eric Gunton ran a prosperous photographic business opposite the Town Hall in Bayeux, until his death. His son Tony lives in Caen and from 1954–61 worked in his father's shop – yet until 2005 never knew of the existence of these extraordinary and unique images. A selection of Corporal Gunton's photographs are on permanent display in the Battle of Normandy Museum in Bayeux, and by the cinema in the D-Day Landing Museum in Arromanches.

No.32 Graves Registration Unit under Captain William Richards OBE and his deputy, 33-year-old Lieutenant (later Captain) Nathaniel Attwood Allen, was destined for Bayeux. It left Easton on the Hill, near Stamford, Lincolnshire, on 3 June 1944 for London's Royal Albert Docks, from which it embarked on 8 June in the SS *Fort Wrigley* to arrive off Arromanches on 11 June. After a two-day wait at sea the men came ashore, and by 15 June they were comfortably lodged at the Villa Bon Accueil, No. 3 Boulevard Sadi Carnot, Bayeux. Most would be there until February 1946. Among the men was Corporal Eric Gunton, 41 (see right), who, like many of his comrades in this work, was over age for front-line duty. He would remain here until 5 November 1945 when he was posted to a nearby civilian internment camp.

In the picture on the left, No.32 GRU headquarters neighbours the huge Villa Lesage (shown in blue): Lesage was the owner of the civilian headstone factory. On 23 June, only 700m (765 yards) away from the future war cemetery site, men bathe and wash clothes in the River Aure. But death was never far off: the hospital returns tell us that some men died of Weil's disease – caused by bacteria in the polluted water and carried by rats – while many wounded died a terrible death from the Normandy soil heavily laden with tetanus spores when no life-saving serums were available.

A rough fate awaited 18-year-old Driver Eddie Saunders (3.C.23) who died on 2 August. Two days earlier he broke his neck diving into a pond, hitting his head on the bottom – a reminder that many of these men were no more than a short step away from being skylarking boys.

> 'We therefore commit his body to the ground,
> Earth to earth, ashes to ashes, dust to dust …'
>
> THE BOOK OF COMMON PRAYER

Burial and exhumation

It was not the function of Registration Units to dig graves, but on 14 July Captain Richards had left instructions that unit labour was to be used as a temporary measure and French labour was to be recruited. The French, who worked both here and at Ryes, often brought to work their own spades and shovels, finding them better adapted to the task than standard British Army issue! (The shortage of labour at Tilly and Hottot-les-Bagues cemeteries was to lead to burials being diverted to Bayeux.)

There were never enough men in the GRUs – only ten men and three officers each normally, but the special status accorded to No.32 GRU for photography and cross painting meant that it was double the size, and engineers and pioneers, as well as a large number of French civilians, helped them out. All burials and exhumations had to be overseen by an officer, and usually took place without ceremony. Provided with a camera and reels of film by the Army, Corporal Eric Gunton was given extraordinary access to the grim, intimate routines that lie behind the mortal remains under every headstone in the beautiful cemeteries we

A military chaplain, in his raincoat and clutching the Book of Common Prayer, carries out the burial service. He is accompanied by Corporal Rene Parsons on the right (see also page 15). This hasty interment in Plot 5, Row 5 is for an unknown soldier. Shrouds were unusual: it may be that the body was deemed to be contagious, since this plot, along with Plots 1 to 4, was a hospital burial area.

see today. His photographs make all too gruesomely clear the conditions in which the men brought human remains to the surface. Below we see Captain Ingolby sifting through unearthed body parts for clues to identity; the two French labourers to his right can also be seen in the picture on the left, struggling to heave out another body from the clinging mud.

The autumn of 1944 was dull, wet and cold, and the men were only allowed to bring one pair of Army boots to Normandy, boots which were notoriously pervious to the wet. The unsavoury, caustic liquid cocktail that burials released in such wet conditions led to a demand for families to send rubber boots from the UK – and not just for those working in the Graves Service.

> **Private Alan Moore, age 22 in 1944, was in Army maintenance at nearby Audrieu, and 35 years a gardener for the Commonwealth War Graves Commission; today aged 84, he lives with his wife in Bayeux. He recalls: 'After our honeymoon [in 1946] we got a lift back from Orfières in a three-ton Bedford truck – and there were bodies in the back on their way to Bayeux to be reburied there.'**

Grave concentration

The first batch of unpainted, pressed, galvanized metal crosses for the Graves Registration Units was delivered in a three-ton truck during the first week of August. On 14 August the permanent bypass was opened, and the temporary bypass, which had served for five weeks, fell into disuse. We can see a considerable degree of order had been imposed by the time this photograph (right) was taken: each grave now has its metal cross and a tamped rectangular mound, and the plots are surrounded by hardcore paths. The battle had passed, leaving behind the urgent need to begin concentration – bringing bodies into the permanent cemetery from the outlying countryside – before poor weather set in to deteriorate human remains further and make identification, digging and transport more difficult.

Grave Concentration Units were better equipped and more substantial at 60 men apiece than the Registration Units – No.39 GCU began its work on

In the foreground, the empty slots of Row F await their occupants: grave 1 is out of shot, by the fence; grave 26 is in front of that of Colonel L.F. Hancock.

This photograph, taken by air reconnaissance on 1 August, shows the cross of the central mall of the cemetery, and the new bypass constructed right round the town. Today the abrupt turn in the road envelops the De Gaulle memorial.

1 Temporary bypass and pipelines split here
2 Station road used for bypass
3 Permanent bypass (south)
4 Bayeux Cemetery
5 N13 to Isigny
6 Site of De Gaulle memorial (1954)
7 No.20 BGH
8 Permanent bypass (north)
9 N13 to Caen

14 October 1944. Captain H. Ingolby MBE set up his headquarters in the Maibre sawmills, the huge roof of which is visible on page 11 between nos. 16 and 20. The Maibre sawmills – demolished in 2006 – manufactured coffins, and their own busy funeral parlour can be seen on page 2. In two weeks, 98 concentration burials were carried out into Bayeux, and the unit would work here until November 1945, when it moved on to Isselhorst in Germany.

In contrast to the random order of the American concentrations into Saint Laurent and Saint James, the order of re-interment into British cemeteries tells us much, although the logic behind it is often obscure. It took five years for the Commonwealth War Graves Commission to digitize the fragile paper burial records of every one of the 1,695,178 men in its care, when it became possible to throw more light on them.

Plot 2, Row F, in the foreground above, shows the first concentration burials in this section being prepared; the freshly cut slots will be filled in two stages, beginning by the fence. Five sappers – (grave F1) Sergeant Len Scott from Durham, (F2) Sapper Bob Cook, 20, from Greenwich, (F3) the driver Pat Collier, 25, from

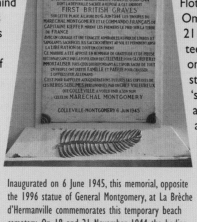

Inaugurated on 6 June 1945, this memorial, opposite the 1996 statue of General Montgomery, at La Brèche d'Hermanville commemorates this temporary beach cemetery. On 18 and 21 November 1944 the bodies were moved from here to Bayeux, Plot 11, Row C. British soldiers who died on D-Day can be found concentrated into Plots 10, 11, 12 and 15.

Lower Parkstone, Dorset, (F4) Sapper Jim Weyman, 37, from Hampstead and (F5) Lance Corporal Harold Bordycott, 30, from Accrington, Lancashire – were killed or mortally wounded as their vehicle drove over a mine on 5 October: Bordycott was brought here directly for burial; his comrades died two days later in a military hospital. The rest of the row would be filled on 10 November when the British bodies buried in the American cemeteries at Colleville and Sainte Mère Eglise were brought in. These would include bodies (F8, 9, 11, 13) originally recovered from the sea – along with just 20 survivors – by two cutters of the US Coast Guard Rescue Flotilla on 20 July, brought ashore at Omaha and buried at Saint Laurent on 21 July. A total of 144 crew – mostly teenagers – and 11 officers lost their lives on board the destroyer HMS *Isis* when it struck a mine (or possibly a human 'suicide' torpedo). The dead and missing are recorded in Portsmouth Cathedral, and the missing on the Chatham Naval Memorial. A mine also blew up HMS *Motor Minesweeper 1019*, killing its two crew members (F23, 24).

Two airmen (F12, 17), shot down over the Cherbourg peninsula in 1942 and buried in churchyards, were brought here at the same time as those bodies from Colleville-Saint-Laurent.

'Found that there had been a misunderstanding and that in the meantime the mayor had agreed to a bypass road being made through the military cemetery. Finally it was agreed to turn the military cemetery half right and forward so as to have the entrance on the new road. This was agreed to by Civil Affairs, the Mayor [Elie Dodeman], the Town Architect and Lt Colonel Lloyd, Commander Royal Engineers, who is building the road. The latter was very helpful and nice in difficult circumstances.'

MAJOR C.E. LUGARD

The entrance to the cemetery

1 July 1944: men of No. 32 GRU (above) are in Monsieur Gautier's field, pegging out and digging what will become the largest British cemetery of the Second World War in France. The field site entrance in this photograph – just visible as a worn track in the hedgerow – is directly on the other side of the road from the walled civilian cemetery (see page 10). The future war cemetery was designated for 5,661 graves on 28 June 1944 by Major C.E. Lugard, officer in charge of all 2nd Army Grave Registrations in Normandy. Men were still being buried when giant earthmovers, transferred from constructing airfields, burst through the hedgerow and barged straight across the cemetery, destroying the municipal tennis courts in their path: a new road was under way, forcing a change in the original plan.

Below, one of the GRU men looks perplexed and scratches his head, standing where it has now been decided the future central mall will be, in the neighbouring field belonging to Madame Lebailly.

28 September 1944: 'The constant downpour of rain makes work of this unit almost impossible. Photography is at a halt, graves at the permanent cemeteries are filling with water ... great difficulties experienced with transport on roads already thick with mud made it increasingly obvious that the open type of trucks allocated to the unit for the performance of registering graves are unsuitable.'

The wisdom of building a new permanent road around Bayeux was apparent. The workforce (above) was tasked with levelling the pathways around each section ready to receive the hardcore. On 26 September the fence was erected by Engineers and the first loads of hardcore for the paths around each section arrived two days later.

7 November 1944: with the central mall complete, a stout wooden gate (below) was erected, with 'British Cemetery' carved in gothic lettering. The rain continued all through the month of November, and towards the end of the month exhumations and reburials almost stopped altogether as the slots were filling with water. In the western front, between the beginning of November and mid-December, the British Second Army advanced a mere 16kms (10 miles): the wettest weather in 80 years did much to contribute to the war dragging into 1945.

> *'I do not suppose that at any moment of history has the agony of the world been so great or widespread. Tonight the sun goes down on more suffering than ever before in the world.'*
> WINSTON CHURCHILL AT YALTA, TO HIS DAUGHTER, 6 FEBRUARY 1945

To absent friends

An appalling autumn was followed by a worse winter, which began punctually enough on 19 December, bringing with it plunging temperatures, bitterly cold northerly gales, freezing fog and, in January, snow, culminating in the very heavy snowfalls at the end of the month recorded in these photographs.

Locating bodies and breaking the frozen ground became extremely difficult, but the concentration burials went on. Beginning on 18 November (out of La Brèche d'Hermanville) Plots 10, 11, 14 and 15 were created at this time, concentrating the D-Day casualties into Plot 10; the dates of death in these four sections are for June 1944, with the exception of some graves in Plot 15, Rows J to M.

Elsewhere in France, the Battle of the Bulge in the Ardennes was being fought in equally miserable conditions, and worse.

LEFT: On Christmas Day 1944 the most poignant toast across the English-speaking world was 'to absent friends'. Indeed for millions of men, women and children of many nationalities, Christmas 1943 had been their last ever. Christmas 1944 would be the final one of the war, and for it No.32 GRU prepared their own Christmas card: at the bottom can be made out Eric Gunton's signature.

> '**The prospect of winter in Normandy seemed bleak. We were sick of mud for a bedroom carpet, sick of bathing in a tin box, sick of having nowhere to hang our clothes. This bout of self-pity was cut short by the arrival of Pioneers to put up Nissen huts in place of the tents. At last we had a real bathroom with hot showers and a place to do our ironing, a place to wash hair, and a cast-iron stove that glowed red-hot in the middle of each hut.**'
> SISTER BRENDA MCBRYDE

It is easy to imagine the men responding to a whistle from the GCU tent, announcing a 'nice hot cuppa tea'. This image, frozen in time, is indicative of Gunton's artistry in capturing an ephemeral moment.

A man in No.32 GRU enjoys a snowball fight in the courtyard at the back of their headquarters, the Villa Bon Accueil (No.3 Boulevard Sadi Carnot). The courtyard backs onto the present Tapestry coach park.

In the January snow, a lorry has stopped at the entrance and the bearers carry their sad, flag-draped burden to its last resting place.

'I came back from Germany on 6 May 1945. I worked in 9 or 10 cemeteries. We scratched up the men's details with bits of broken glass. We dug the graves when the lorries brought in the bodies. I remember one which had been buried in three different places before; this was his fourth cemetery. They arrived in Army blankets, I never saw a coffin. There was no ceremony.'

M GIBERT, 22 IN 1945

1945: the price of victory ... and solidarity

On 5 October 1944 the first three Imperial War Graves Commission (IWGC) representatives had arrived at Arromanches to pick up the pieces of the Commission's work in Europe forcibly abandoned in 1940. Their first task had been to visit the 1,375 First World War cemeteries with their 400kms (250 miles) of headstones in Northern France and Belgium: it came as a surprise to find that while there was neglect, the damage was not so great as feared. Where damage was identified, it became known as 'honourable scars'. Also, where churchyard burials had been carried out by the French under German supervision, airmen lost over occupied territories had in general been interred according to the rules of war: indeed for propaganda purposes the Germans had been keen that this should be seen to be done.

The IWGC set themselves up in a Nissen hut in Saint Aubin sur Mer with little more than a typewriter, orange crates for filing cabinets and a shell-case for boiling tea: they even received their petrol and rations courtesy of the Army. In December 1944, IWGC officers visited Bayeux to inspect the cemeteries and give useful advice to the Army on how they might begin to beautify the different sites and take future landscaping projects into account. In the case of Bayeux, areas behind Plots 2 and 3 were allocated for the future memorials, visitors' buildings and plantations – thereby reducing the potential size of the cemetery site from the planned 5,661 to 4,700: eventually there would be a total of 3,602 identified British graves and 335 British unknowns. There are also today: 3 Canadian unknowns, 178 identified Canadian burials, 17 Australians, 8 New Zealanders, 1 South African, 25 Poles (including 1 unknown), 7 Russians, 2 Czechs, 2 Italians, 3 French – and 465 Germans, 49 of whom are unknown: a total of 4,648 graves. Confusion often rises over the total because a further 8 men, all in the Merchant Navy, did not meet the Commonwealth War Graves criteria of what constitutes a 'war grave'.

A central mall has been created, visible in the aerial photo on page 18, the gate (1) giving onto the bypass, each section framed by a limestone hardcore path (2) to ease access. The communal cemetery with its evergreen trees (3), the Lesage monumental masonry works (4), the porcelain factory (5), the pediment of the sub-prefecture (6) and the cathedral spires (7) behind the GCU tent (8) form the reference points for many of the Gunton photographs in this book.

The churchyard at Saint Martin des Entrées, on the N13 just before Bayeux – one of 209 in Normandy with Commonwealth interments – has a single Commonwealth war grave. Spitfire Pilot Officer William Kennedy Ferguson, 21, of the Royal Canadian Air Force, basketball and baseball player, lover of jazz , poker and girls, was killed on 15 January 1943 crashing his plane near the railway line at Damigny (where the new ring road goes over the railway). The horrific scene was witnessed by three locals who gathered up his dismembered body to await collection, but when the Germans arrived 48 hours later the obscene and public manner in which the remains were forced into an over-short coffin stoked the outrage, and on 18 January 250 civilians out of Bayeux and the surrounding villages descended upon the cemetery, laden with tricolor wreaths and flowers. When the Germans turned up for what they had hoped would be a discreet military ceremony, the officer gave the mourners just three minutes to remove the floral tributes, and the IDs of 132 of those present were confiscated. Following brutal interrogations, 10 were sent to Mauthausen and Buchenwald, four of them youngsters arrested in their English lesson. Four of the 10 never returned.

> **'In the course of my pilgrimage, I have many times asked myself whether there can be more potent advocates of peace upon earth, through the years to come, than this massed multitude of silent witnesses to the desolation of war.'**
>
> KING GEORGE V IN 1922, ON HIS FIRST VISIT TO A WAR CEMETERY IN FRANCE

The Bayeux British Cemetery

In Normandy during February 1945, the weather turned to mild, even warm conditions; spring came early and the above-average temperatures persisted into the summer, allowing for good progress in disinterments and concentrations – and to ending the war.

Compare the picture below with that on page 1: the house (which is still there today) on the bend in the Littry road that runs behind the old elms is a useful reference point – it also appears on pages 10 and 20. The worn ground shows where the GCU tent stood, with its drainage channels. On 22 February the officers and clerks of No. 39 GCU moved into the spacious Langlois Farm 275m (300 yards) away to work in more comfortable conditions (see page 11; the farm is halfway between nos. 10 and 16). The bypass has now gone eerily quiet, allowing a man to walk his goats undisturbed alongside the perimeter fence, beyond which the work of concentration and reburial goes on.

In the Second World War, the proportion of British dead (326,000 military and 62,000 civilian fatalities) to the United Kingdom population was five times greater than that of American dead to its population. Entered into with France on a matter of principle, the war had been fought by the UK for longer than any other country, endured from its declaration on 3 September 1939 to its end in the Pacific on 2 September 1945. The conflict left the country, with its allies, victorious – but exhausted and bankrupt.

> **'Churchill feared that the world would soon forget the scale of Britain's sacrifice. He told the Cabinet Office: "Get me the best figures available of the losses sustained by the English [UK citizens] in this war ...". The Prime Minister received in response statistics of relative mortality among the Western allied nations of the Second World War: by April 1945 one in 165 UK citizens had died, one in 130 Londoners, one in 385 Australians, one in 385 Canadian, one in 175 New Zealanders and one in 775 Americans. The Western Allies possessed no idea of how many Russians had been killed, and no one in Moscow was likely to tell them.'**
>
> MAX HASTINGS, *ARMAGEDDON*

BAYEUX
BRITISH
CEMETERY

On 15 November 1944 a three-ton truck full of personnel on the way to the cinema in Bayeux was in a road accident: the driver, Norman Norton, 23, and Private John Marchant, 34, both suffered fatal injuries. Their unit Captain lays flowers on their graves (2.D.13 and 12) the next day. With the battle over, the majority of deaths in Normandy were caused by traffic accidents and undetected mines.

Simplify me when I'm dead

Remember me when I am dead
and simplify me when I'm dead.

As the processes of earth
strip off the colour and the skin:
take the brown hair and blue eye

and leave me simpler than at birth,
when hairless I came howling in
as the moon came in the cold sky.

Of my skeleton perhaps,
so stripped, a learned man will say
'He was of such a type and intelligence,' no more.

Thus when in a year collapse
particular memories, you may
deduce, from the long pain I bore

the opinions I held, who was my foe
and what I left, even my appearance
but incidents will be no guide.

Time's wrong-way telescope will show
a minute man ten years hence
and by distance simplified.

Through that lens see if I seem
substance or nothing: of the world
deserving mention or charitable oblivion,

not by momentary spleen
or love into decision hurled,
leisurely arrive at an opinion.

Remember me when I am dead
and simplify me when I'm dead.

KEITH DOUGLAS

Having driven his Sherman tank through Bayeux on 7 June, Captain Keith Douglas, 24, perhaps the most promising young poet of the Second World War, was killed two days later by a shell exploding close above his head – leaving no mark on his body. He was buried in a field the next day by Padre Skinner and later concentrated to the nearby cemetery of Tilly (I.E.2).

Since 1944 a local tradition has been for French families to 'adopt' graves, receive next of kin and lay floral tributes. From the age of 12, Marie-Ange Françoise, whose family lived on the Littry road and whose father worked as a gravedigger, has honoured the memory of several of the men buried in Bayeux, including: top/left, Warrant Officer 'Stan' Strachan, killed 24 August 1944 age 36 (28:G:10); top/right, Corporal Arthur Harris, killed 31 August 1944 age 23 (28:G:11); centre/below, Captain Milton John Francis, killed 8 August 1944 age 30 (4.B.20).

Acknowledgements

Text by William Jordan, Historian and Lecturer, since 1991 Guide-Conférencier des Monuments Historiques et des Sites in Caen. (www.normandylandingbeaches.com).
Edited by Gill Knappett.
Pictures researched by William Jordan and Chris Hall.
Designed by Tim Noel-Johnson.

The photographs are reproduced as follows: CWGC ifc top; Marie-Ange Françoise 2, 3t, 28–ibc (men); Eric Gunton © Nadia Gilbert 4b, 4–5t, 6, 14–15t, 16b, 16–17t, 22–23ct; Eric Gunton © Ray Glover 12–13b, 17b, 23r; Eric Gunton © Ray Glover/Jackie Henderson ifc–1b; Eric Gunton © Jackie Henderson fc, bc, pp14–15t, 14–15 background, 18–19t, 20–21 all inc background, 22l, 22–23b, 24–25t, 26-27b, 27t; IWM 3b, 5b, 6, 7, 8, 9 both, 11b inset, 12t, 13t, 14b; William Jordan 19b, 25b, 28–ibc (graves); Rene Lefetey 15t; TARA (The Aerial Reconnaissance Archives), Keele University, UK 10 inset, 10–11 main, 11t inset, 18b.

This book has been made possible by the generosity of Jackie Henderson, Ray Glover and Nadia Gilbert who have granted permission for the use of all the considerable archive of original Gunton negatives in their possession. Special thanks also to: Chris Hall for his detailed archive research in the UK, and his detailed graphic work on the aerial photos on pp10–11 and 18; Professeur Remy Desquesnes of the Bayeux Museum for reading the text; Tony Gunton, Marie-Ange Françoise, Ray Glover, Alan Moore, Katia Boyadjian, Rene Lefetey and Claudia Goodfellow for their help. The author is indebted to the Battle of Normandy Museum in Bayeux and the Commonwealth War Graves Commission for their support in the Gunton project.

Quotes are used by permission as follows: ifc (M Leclerc), pp2 (Mlle Bouve/Mme Ratel), 5 (M Ledolley), 17 (Alan Moore), 24 (M Gibert) all © William Jordan; p3 (Mlle Dubois) Vie quotidienne 1940–1945 © Mme Huet/lycée Alain Chartier, Regards culturels en Bessin; pp5, 6–7, 7, 12 (from The Man Who Worked on Sundays by Leslie Skinner) © Ken Ewing; p5 (Lance Corporal Seaman, from Thank God and the Infantry by John Lincoln) © Sutton Publishing Ltd; p5 (John Cropper, from Dad's War by Andy Cropper) © Andy Cropper; p6 (John Semken) © from BBC Radio 4 Padre Skinner's War; p8 (from The Guns of Normandy by George Blackburn) © McClelland & Stewart Ltd, Toronto; pp20, 21 © The National Archives, Kew; pp22, 26 (Winston Churchill) reproduced by permission of Curtis Brown Ltd, London, on behalf of The Estate of Winston Churchill; p26 (from Armageddon by Max Hastings) © Macmillan, London; bc (John Maxwell Edmonds) © V&A Publications; p28 'Simplify me when I'm dead' from Collected Poems by Keith Douglas © Faber & Faber.

Other quotes: pp3, 8, 9, 22 from A Nurse's War by Brenda McBryde; p13 from Quiet Heroines by Brenda McBryde; pp6, 7, 8 from 11 Men and a Scalpel by Major J.B. Hillsman. Every effort has been made to trace copyright holders and the publisher will be pleased to rectify any omissions in future editions.

Publication in this form © Jarrold Publishing 2006. No part of this publication may be reproduced by any means without the permission of Jarrold Publishing and the copyright holders.

Pitkin Guides is an imprint of Jarrold Publishing, Norwich.

Printed in Great Britain.
ISBN-10: 1-84165-176-1
ISBN-13: 978-1-84165-176-7

1/06

SUGGESTED WEBSITES
To locate Commonwealth burials worldwide go to the Commonwealth War Graves Commission website: www.cwgc.org
To support British veterans or find out more about The Royal British Legion go to www.britishlegion.org.uk

When you go home

Tell them of us and say

For your tomorrow

We gave our today

PITKIN

ISBN 1-84165-176-1